My name is

My name is

Yoshiko

YOSHIKO SUSAN KAWAGUCHI MATSUMOTO

with Pamela Varma Brown

Write Path, LLC
Kapaa, Kauai, Hawaii

Cover design: Aaron Yadao,
Ink Spot Printing, Kauai, Hawaii
Book interior: Write Path, LLC
Title font: Linotype Zapfino designed by Hermann Zapf
Text font: Minion Pro

Cover photo:
Yoshiko Susan Kawaguchi Matsumoto on her wedding day,
May 3, 1947, in Chicago.

First Printing: December 2015

ISBN: 978-0-9856983-8-6 (Paperback)
ISBN: 978-0-9856983-9-3 (ebook)
Library of Congress Control Number: 2015959081

To my family & friends

May this book be my legacy
to remind the world that
all people are created equal.

Acknowledgments

$\mathcal{I}$ am grateful to my father for his spirit and sense of adventure in coming to the United States from Japan in 1905. He barely knew how to speak English but he knew farming. Somehow he had the faith to know he would be all right. He set the groundwork for my mother, the four of his children, and all of our children, to enjoy life in this country.

Thank you to Pamela Varma Brown for her time and expertise writing my life story from our long talks, poring over my many diaries in which I wrote my memories, and gathering photos from my many photo albums.

Thank you also to my niece, Janice Yoshihara Olson, who put together as a gift for me in 2013 a wonderful booklet of my life, from which some of the material for this book has been taken.

As we say in Hawaii, *mahalo* (thank you) to everyone who proofread this book: Steven Geyer, Andy Johnston, Jan Rentz and Viviane Stein.

And thank you, dear reader, for coming on this journey with me.

Yoshiko Susan Kawaguchi Matsumoto
Yoshiko Susan Kawaguchi Matsumoto
December 2015

Table of Contents

Acknowledgments		vii
Chapter 1	A New Life	1
Chapter 2	Growing Up on a Farm	5
Chapter 3	My Name is Yoshiko	13
Chapter 4	Parisian School of Fashion Arts	19
Chapter 5	The End of Life as We Knew It	23
Chapter 6	The FBI Visits Us	27
Chapter 7	Living in a Horse Stall	29
Chapter 8	Rohwer Internment Camp: Gaman	39
Chapter 9	Life Behind Barbed Wire	43
Chapter 10	Rejoining America	49
Chapter 11	Becoming Susan	55
Chapter 12	Mr. Tom T. Matsumoto	63

Chapter 13	On Our Own	71
Chapter 14	Hawaiian Mailman in Chicago	79
Chapter 15	Rachel	83
Chapter 16	All in a Day's Work	89
Chapter 17	Learning to Drive #1	93
Chapter 18	Returning to Downey	95
Chapter 19	Learning to Drive #2	99
Chapter 20	Ferndale Nursery	101
Chapter 21	Tom's Homecoming to Kauai	105
Chapter 22	Kindness to Strangers	111
Chapter 23	Apology 45 Years Later	115
Chapter 24	Aloha, My Dear Husband	117
Chapter 25	94 Years Old and Counting!	123

My name is
Yoshiko

Chapter 1
A New Life

It is only now that I am a 94-year-old woman, I realize how brave my father was to come to America from Japan by himself in 1905. I wonder if he still would have made the journey if he had known that after living in the United States for almost four decades, he, his wife and four children would be imprisoned behind barbed wire for two-and-a-half years, simply because of our Japanese ancestry.

Knowing my father's ability to make the best of any situation, he probably would have come anyway.

My father, Yoshigoro Kawaguchi, grew up very poor in the mountains of Wakayama, Japan, where he was a farmer. At the age of 28, he boarded a ship bound for Vancouver, Canada. Upon arriving, he settled in Seattle, Washington.

Dad's good fortune began almost as soon as he started working in Seattle, when he met the Robeson family, who owned a candy store. The Robesons were relatives of a man named Hiram Johnson, an up-and-coming politician who became California's governor in 1911.

When the Robesons relocated to Los Angeles to live near Mr. Johnson, they invited Dad to come with them. He got work on the Johnson family's large farm, where they grew hay and beans. Father's job was cleaning the barn and horse stalls. It was not a very nice job, and he had to wake at 4:30 each morning to work. But it paid well: $150 per month which was very good in those days.

The Johnsons must have liked my father a lot because they also provided him a place to live, health insurance and food. Over the 15 years he worked for them, they also paid for his trips to Japan three times.

The Johnsons apparently could not pronounce my father's name, Yoshigoro, so they gave him the name Henry. Dad kept that name until he passed away in 1967.

Even though Dad was a hard worker, he saved very little of the money that he earned for himself. He sent most of his wages to his brother in Japan to help support their family. But after 15 years, he had saved enough money to return to Japan to get a wife.

My mother, Okane Kawaguchi, was born in 1899 in Japan and grew up near the Pacific Ocean. She told me that as a little girl, she always enjoyed watching the large ships from the United States that came into port near her home.

As the youngest of three daughters, in a family that also had one son, my mother knew she was last in line.

*Me with my mother, when
I was about two years old.*

Anything the family owned would be given to her brother. As a teenager, my mother worked in a button factory. She knew there had to be more in life, and agreed to come to the United States with my father.

My father brought my mother to America in 1920. When they arrived in the port of Washington, the authorities were initially going to deport my mother because of an issue with her eyes. But thanks to Mr. Hiram Johnson, she was admitted to the United States. I don't know exactly what Mr. Johnson said or did, but my father told us that Mr. Johnson had intervened. What a blessing that my father had worked for someone so well-connected.

My parents found a small apartment in Seattle. Years later my father told me their apartment had been so small that at Christmastime, they had to tie the Christmas tree to their bed headboard. Typical of my father, he made the most of whatever they had, no matter how little it was.

At first my mother found it challenging to adjust to life in America, especially because she never learned to speak English well. Over time she learned that people liked her, regardless of how she communicated with them.

I was born in 1921. My parents named me Yoshiko, which means "good child" in Japanese.

I don't know what my Dad did to pay the rent while we lived in Seattle, but my mom told me she cut cabbage in the cold and snow. I'm sure it was a hard job. My father did all the cooking until Mom slowly learned how to use the kerosene stove.

I wish I knew more about my parents' early life, but when you are growing up, you only think of playing.

Chapter 2

Growing Up on a Farm

After about three years in Seattle, Dad decided he wanted to return to Southern California because it was warmer and it was much easier to farm there. Farming was the only real skill he had.

We took a train to Los Angeles. My father told me that I cried so loudly on the train, he wished he could just cover me up!

Once in Los Angeles, my father found a small apartment for us, and got himself a job at an Owl Drug Store, a chain in those years. Although his reading and writing of English was basic, he could read the labels on the jars of pills on the shelves. To make ends meet, he also worked as a janitor, cleaning the store.

Every time he had a day off, Dad went to the employment office seeking farm work. Jobs were scarce, but he was willing to work hard.

At first, my mother found work in a factory, hand-stitching lace for beautiful handkerchiefs. The factory was nearby so she would walk to work, taking me and my younger sister, Yoneko, with her, pick up the work, and bring it home. Those handkerchiefs were so beautiful with her handmade lace and butterflies. I am sure they were not used to blow your nose!

Finally my father landed a job on a farm with the Ikegami family in Downey, 13 miles southeast of Los Angeles. It was just what my father was hoping for. The farm was quite large, maybe 50 acres. My father helped them grow cabbage, cauliflower, potatoes, corn and tomatoes, according to the season, and also tended to the many fruit trees that were already on the land before he arrived.

Today Downey is a busy city with a population of about 115,000, set within the larger Southern California region that is home to some 22 million people. But back then, it was very rural: all orange groves and farms as far as the eye could see. In those days, the sky was so clear and blue, we could see the top of Los Angeles City Hall from the farm. Temperatures all summer were between 75 and 80 degrees Fahrenheit, and there was very little rain. It was a perfect climate for year-round farming.

When we relocated to Downey, we had only a few belongings and did not own a vehicle, so we moved there by taxi. I was 6 or 7 years old.

This farm became the center of our family's existence for more than a dozen years. The work was difficult and exhausting. I grew up watching my parents and learning that hard work was our duty.

The Ikegamis provided us a small one-room, single-walled house attached to their home. As you can imagine, there was no space for a refrigerator, nor could my parents have afforded one. We had only the basics: two double beds, one for my parents and one for my sister and me, all four of us sleeping in that one room. We also had a round table and one chair. In those days few people had radios, and this was long before televisions became commonplace in homes.

We didn't have indoor plumbing. Moveable wooden toilets were placed over holes outdoors. When the holes beneath them were filled, new holes were dug, the toilets were moved and the old holes were covered with dirt.

Our family in 1930 in front of a vehicle owned by the Ikegamis. I was about 8 years old.

For bathing, we shared a *furo*, a Japanese-style outdoor bathtub, with the Ikegamis. The *furo* was a large metal tub, heated by a fire underneath. *Furos* were very common in those years in rural areas where Japanese people lived. Before stepping into the *furo*, we always rinsed ourselves off with cold water from a large bucket, so the nice warm water in the *furo* remained clean long enough for everyone in our two households to enjoy a cleansing bath.

The work that my parents did was back-breaking, like most farm work, but I never heard either of them complain about anything. On the contrary, they seemed grateful to have found a big farm where there was plenty of work to do.

Farm work was especially hard on their bodies during cauliflower season. Stooping low through row after row of cauliflower plants, they peeled the leaves back and peeked inside each one to see if there was a small white cauliflower head growing. When there was, they tied a piece of string on the plant to easily find it when it was fully grown.

When harvest time came, my parents followed a high wooden cart pulled between the rows by one horse and cut the cauliflower heads, throwing them into the cart. The harvested cauliflower was packed in crates. At 8 p.m. every evening, a man from the 9th Street Market in Los Angeles came to pick up the crates, and brought them to the place where they were sold.

After cauliflower season was over, my father leveled the ground with a wooden leveler pulled by two horses, then created rows in which the next crop would be planted. I often wondered how many miles my father walked while cultivating each row, especially during the summer when he worked from 6 a.m. to 6 p.m.

During potato season, Mother stood in the barn for hours, cutting the eyes off old potatoes and placing them in a gunny sack that was nailed to the table. Later the eyes were planted in the soil that Dad had prepared. As a girl, I learned to trap gophers to keep them from eating the baby potatoes as they began to grow.

While Mom prepared the potato eyes for planting, my sister Yoneko and I whiled away many hours watching chickens lay their eggs in bales of hay that were stacked in the barn. We loved to search for and find those eggs.

We children had no toys, but we always found something to do to keep busy. We'd pick up stones and twigs or whatever we could find on the farm. When we wanted a snack, my sisters and I usually ate plain rice balls.

After potato season, it became tomato season, and the months-long process of growing, tending, harvesting and boxing was repeated. Overripe tomatoes went into tall cannery cans that were sent to the factory, where they were made into ketchup and other tomato-based products.

One day, do not ask me how, I crawled into one of the long tomato cannery cans. I must have been wondering if I could fit inside the can, but then I could not get out! Mom couldn't get me out either, so someone had to cut the can in half to release me. Mom was so angry. She chased me around our small house and scolded me. I was only 7 or 8 years old and had not known any better.

My parents were fortunate that the Ikegamis had so much work for them, but there were times, between harvest and replanting, when it stopped. During those dry spells, my parents worked on other people's farms.

During one such spell, our family temporarily relocated to a house in Orange County, where my youngest sister Yoshino was born.

I worked sometimes, too, at another Japanese family's roadside stand selling carrots, turnips, green onions, spinach, beets, cabbage and strawberries. These are some of the prices we had at that stand:

- Small head of lettuce   1 cent
- Large head of lettuce   5 cents
- Three nice bunches of spinach 5 cents
- Basket of strawberries   5 cents
- Loaf of unsliced bread   5 cents
- Big box of oranges   35 cents

After a handful of years, our one-room house that the Ikegamis provided for us finally felt too small, and when my parents could afford it, Dad found a much larger home for our family. With three bedrooms, a bathroom, kitch-

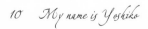

en, dining room, living room and porch, it seemed like a mansion to us!

We still did not have a refrigerator, so we stored our meat in the bathtub where it was cool. (We had a regular American-style tub in this house.) To get hot water to do our dishes, we had to heat water on a kerosene stove. There was a small dairy farm right next door, so every morning Yoneko would go to the dairy and pick up a quart of milk.

Our furniture consisted of whatever well-worn items the former tenant had left behind, along with Mother's large steamer trunk in which she brought her things from Japan when she first arrived in the United States. The former tenant had also left an old set of encyclopedias that we enjoyed studying.

There was a lot of open space around this house. My sisters and I had fun flying kites behind our new home. We were only half a block away, down a dirt road, from the main highway. On the other side of the road, a Japanese farmer was raising strawberries on five acres. When the hot Santa Ana winds blew, the tumbleweeds would come flying from everywhere, hitting our legs like small, stinging rocks.

Dad installed a mailbox on the highway so we could receive mail. Every Christmas he made us wait for the mailman to give him an envelope with some money in it as a Christmas gift. Isn't it funny that when I grew up, I married a man who became a mailman?

The owner of the house was a woman named Mrs. Hope. She came from Los Angeles each month to collect the $15 rent. She wanted to sell the house to us for $1,500 but in those days, Japanese nationals were not allowed to own any property in the U.S. We loved our new home, and were grateful that Mrs. Hope agreed to rent to us.

For the first time since before I was born, my parents had their own bedroom, and soon our baby brother, Yoshio, came along. We didn't have a telephone, so I had gone to the neighbor's house to call the doctor to deliver the baby. Yoshio was so cute and precious. He had two dimples. Yoneko and I slept in one double bed and once our brother was born, our sister Yoshino shared her bed with him.

I don't know if my parents had gotten a raise working for the Ikegamis, or if they had simply saved their money over the years, but somehow we found ourselves with our family's first vehicle: a 1930 Ford. It was the kind that had to be cranked to start it. As children, we cherished that car. We cleaned and polished it all the time, and even checked the oil.

Dad was not a good driver. Yoneko always had to sit in the front and tell him when to stop and go, or where to turn. Dad never liked driving from our home in Downey to Los Angeles because he felt unnerved by the large, bus-like streetcars that were part of the city's mass transit system back then.

It must have been very difficult for my parents to provide for all four of us children on their farm wages. But somehow they did it. I think it was because they always had hope.

Chapter 3
My Name is Yoshiko

By the time I was 6 years old and attending school in rural Downey, I still knew how to speak only Japanese, so I was held back two years in school. One day my teacher sent me home with a note that said, "Please teach Yoshiko how to read and speak English."

At that time, my father could speak only broken English and could read just a little bit, but he tried to help me. I brought home a book from school named, "The Little Red Hen." One of the pages said, "This little red hen picked up a grain of rice." Touching a chopstick to each word, Dad said each word out loud to me. But with his accent, this is how he pronounced it: "This lito redo hen peckutoe wheato."

The next day when I went back to class, I thought I could read English and I was so excited. The children all laughed at me. But that's how I started to learn. I thought to myself, "I've got to really learn how to read and write."

I don't know how I eventually figured it out, but I guess I was an ambitious little girl. I practiced and practiced. I must have learned something, because over the years, I have become a voracious reader; I've written volumes in my journals and diaries; and I'm often told that I have very nice penmanship.

Through the years, my father also learned to read and write English better, too. He wrote in beautiful, flowing script. I wish I had kept some of his letters. I also wish I had thought to ask him how he learned, but I didn't think of that until long after he had passed on.

My mom slowly learned to speak English, too, and to write her own name. I was so proud of her.

Little by little, my English speaking got better, as well. Today, at 94 years of age, I speak English fluently and I have lost my Japanese accent completely.

My elementary school was a two-room school-house. In one of the rooms, the first row of students was first-graders (only five of them); the second row was second-graders and the third row was third-graders. The second room was arranged the same way with fourth-, fifth- and sixth-graders. Our desks had inkwells in them. Back in those days, we dipped our pens into a bottle of ink to write.

Our teacher was Mrs. Dean, a wonderful, caring woman. She was so patient as I tried to learn fractions. She helped after school, day after day, until I mastered them.

Mrs. Dean knew that her students' parents were farm

laborers who could not come home until late. Sometimes she brought children to her home after school. We would play games, eat cookies and enjoy cool drinks before she brought us home in the evenings.

Sometimes on rainy days, Mrs. Dean made stew for us in a large pot in the back of our classroom. She would bring the stew meat and somehow we children knew to bring potatoes, carrots, celery, onions or whatever we could. Oh my goodness, it smelled so good, we could hardly wait for lunch! Mrs. Dean even had a cupboard with soup bowls and utensils for us.

The only thing I ever argued with my father about was spending money for typical student activities. One time, when I was in junior high school and he would not give me five cents to buy a chocolate bar or some ice cream at the school student store, I got angry. I decided to go to church and become a nun. Armed with my school-age knowledge, I told my parents, "At least the nuns get to eat ice cream." From that time, I became a church-going person.

My parents were originally Buddhists. We were always so busy on the farm that we went to Buddhist temple in Los Angeles only twice a year. Eventually my mother began reading the Christian Bible, written in Japanese. I guess she noticed a difference between being a Buddhist and being a Christian. My father remained Buddhist. My sister Yoneko and I, we decided, "We're going to be Christians."

As a child, I didn't understand how challenging it was for my parents to support our family. Our parents never let us participate in any school activities or go anywhere with our classmates, like to see movies or other fun events. We had to come home and work on the farm. It was always work, work, work. Even when we were not feeling too well, my dad made us work in the hot sun. I had to wear a long-sleeved shirt and a big Mexican hat to protect my skin.

During the busy strawberry and tomato seasons, we worked from 6 a.m. to 6 p.m., sometimes even until 8 p.m. On Saturdays I frequently worked at a roadside stand that was run by another Japanese family. I earned 25 cents for a 10-hour day.

We never complained and obeyed our parents. In hindsight, I realize they must have needed our help to plant or harvest to keep the farm on schedule, but when I was a girl, I didn't think of that.

We three sisters also took care of our baby brother, since Dad and Mom had such long work hours. At 10 years old, I was cooking rice and preparing dinner when our parents came home from work. My sisters and I were more like little grown-ups, cleaning house, doing laundry and pulling our red wagon to the gas station with our five-gallon gasoline can to be filled with kerosene for our kerosene stove.

As I got older, Mother taught me, "If you have money saved up, you can buy anything." I suppose in retrospect, this is how I became so frugal, so much so that Mother once told me, "If everyone was like you, all the stores would go out of business."

As we became adults, all of this training from our early years became invaluable. Because of our upbringing, we were always able to accept any kind of work and not be afraid of putting in a little effort. We learned we could do anything to survive.

Chapter 4
Parisian School of Fashion Arts

$\mathcal{D}uring$ high school, I had taken one year of book-keeping until my teacher told me, "Yoshiko, one year of bookkeeping is enough for you." I was so accustomed to accepting what other people told me, I didn't argue, though it somehow felt wrong.

After graduating from high school and receiving my diploma, I applied to Woodbury College. But my parents thought that since we were Japanese, I would never be able to get a job.

Mom and Dad said, "We think the best thing for you is to go to sewing school," because at least I could make some money doing piecework from home.

A friend of my parents, Mr. Umeda, ran a thriving barbershop in Los Angeles. He recommended that I attend the same school as his daughter: the Parisian School of Fashion Arts in Los Angeles. It was located upstairs in a building next to an insurance company.

I started school in September 1940. The student fee was $15 per month. That was a lot of money for my parents.

I can't even imagine how many hours of farm labor they had to work to afford my tuition. I was determined to make the most of it.

Going to that fashion school, that's when I grew up. I learned my way around and how to be out in the world on my own. Everything beyond the farm was so new to me.

I woke up at 4 a.m. to get ready for school. Dad would wake earlier than I did to make toast for me. We did not have a toaster, so he would sit at the kerosene stove and brown one side of the bread, then turn it over and brown the other side. The night before, he prepared fresh grapefruits with sugar on top — those were so good. All these years later, I understand how dedicated my father was to creating a life in which education would take me further than either he or my mom were able to go.

Each morning at 6 a.m. I took my seat on a small red bus that held a dozen people, and rode it to the electric train that took me to the 9th Street depot, where I arrived at 8 a.m. From there, I walked the two blocks up to Los Angeles Street, skipping Main Street, where derelicts hung out. My mother had warned me not to talk to strangers.

She told me they had dungeons and if they captured us, we would never see our parents again. So I was very cautious. When I reached Mr. Umeda's barbershop, I would stay there until 8:45, when Mr. Umeda's daughter, Sumiko, and I walked to our school. Classes began at 9 a.m.

When school ended at 3 p.m., I did my whole trip in reverse, finally catching my little red bus that took me back to Downey, getting home about 4:30 p.m. My goodness, it was a full day's job getting back and forth to school. But I loved that school. It was such a different life than working on a farm.

In fashion school I learned how to draft patterns from looking at catalogs, and how to make all sorts of clothing: dresses, blouses and men's jackets. Later we started learning how to sew underpanties and bras. Thanks to the skills I learned at this school, I made many clothes over the years for my sisters, and shirts for my brother, too.

Many of the Japanese girls who attended school with me were from all over the country. I give them credit. In those days, many of the Japanese girls did domestic work for Hollywood movie stars and paid their own way for their education. They did not ask their parents, and of course, most of their parents could not have afforded the cost of any tuition, no matter how small.

As I progressed, my teacher told me I was good enough that she wanted to send me to work at one of the clothing shops or factories on Los Angeles Street, the hub of Southern California's garment district in those years. I was looking forward to that.

But I never got the chance.

Chapter 5
The End of Life as We Knew It

Just before 8 a.m. on the morning of Sunday, December 7, 1941, kamikaze pilots from the country of Japan bombed 16 U.S. Navy ships moored at Pearl Harbor on the Hawaiian island of Oahu, pulling the United States into World War II. I was 10 days shy of my 20th birthday.

Our family was unaware of the attack until my parents came home from the farm that evening and we heard the news on the radio. We were shocked and so sad to learn of the 2,400 Americans killed and another 1,200 wounded.

In a lighter moment, I thought to myself, "Where in the world is Pearl Harbor?" I began reading about Hawaii and what a beautiful place it is. It sounded so exotic. I thought to myself, "Maybe someday I might get to meet someone from Hawaii."

The day after Pearl Harbor was attacked, I went to school, but it was scary. Some of the Japanese were kicked off streetcars and spat on. On First Street in Japantown, people were just rushing around. It was chaos.

I was frightened to make the long journey home that

day. I was able to get home safely, but that was my last day at the Parisian School of Fashion Arts. I was too scared to return. I left all my equipment at school, except one fashion book that for some reason I had brought home with me.

Very soon our new reality began to sink in. We, and all the Japanese families in America, would be looked upon with suspicion because our parents were originally from Japan. My parents were terribly worried. Dad said, "We're all American citizens, but I wonder what is going to happen to us."

The owner of this store in Oakland, Calif., a person of Japanese descent and a graduate of the University of California, placed the "I AM AN AMERICAN" sign across his window the day after Pearl Harbor was bombed. Photographer: Dorothea Lange, March 13, 1942. Courtesy National Archives

Several nights during the next few months, between 10 p.m. and midnight when it was very dark outside, we heard gunshots everywhere around our home. Each time, my father would go to the kitchen window trying to see where the shots were coming from, but it was impossible to see anything in the pitch black. We knew the gunshots were aimed at our house because we were the only Japanese family in our neighborhood. I learned later that rocks had been thrown at some of my Japanese friends' homes in other neighborhoods.

The owner of our house received many threatening letters because we were Japanese. She was feisty, and told the neighbors that we were very nice Japanese people, and if they did not like it, she was going to rent the house to some black people.

Our landlady was one of the first people I ever heard of who stood up to prejudice. We were so grateful to be able to stay in that house. We didn't know that would soon be coming to an end.

Chapter 6
The FBI Visits Us

Shortly after those terrifying nights of gunshots around our home, the word went out among Japanese farmworkers in Southern California that men posing as FBI agents were going house to house, acting like they were investigating Japanese families.

One day I was mopping the kitchen floor when a man showed up unannounced on our doorstep and said he was a *real* FBI agent. He showed us his badge and told us that he had to come inside our house to check everything. He told us that anything from Japan or written in Japanese had to be taken from us and burned.

All six of us sat together in the dining room, so scared and nervous. My mother told my brother, who was about 6 at the time, in Japanese, "When the FBI asks you any questions, don't answer. Just say you don't know."

The FBI agent inspected everything, looking everywhere throughout our home. He even turned over our bed mattresses to see if anything from Japan was hidden there.

We had a phonograph on which we played Japanese

songs. The FBI agent said all the records had to be taken away from us and broken. We kids cried because our favorite children's songs were going to be destroyed.

Even my mother's Christian Bible was confiscated because it was written in Japanese so she could understand it. The FBI man told us the Bible would have to be burned. It was terrible.

After the FBI man left, we were all really scared. We didn't know what was going to happen next.

Chapter 7

Living in a Horse Stall

Over the next few weeks, we began to see governmental notices posted around town announcing that all persons of Japanese ancestry were being "evacuated." We were required to report on April 13, 1942, to a place the government was calling the "Santa Anita Assembly Center."

The notices said that each person could bring only one suitcase with them, just whatever we could carry. We were not told how long we would have to stay at this "assembly center" or what it would be like.

We didn't know what to do with the few things we owned. One of our non-Japanese neighbors agreed to hold our beloved 1930 Ford for us, and also my sewing machine.

It was heartbreaking to watch Japanese men and woman have to walk away from businesses that they had spent years building, with all their belongings left inside their stores. There was no one left to care for the property left behind because the evacuation order affected all Japanese people, about 120,000 of us across the entire nation.

My father said, "Oh my goodness, we didn't do anything bad."

*Farewell notice posted on the window of Iseri Pharmacy in the
Little Tokyo area of Los Angeles two days before
all Japanese in the area were required to report to the
Santa Anita Assembly Center at the Santa Anita Racetrack, where,
unbeknownst to them, they would be imprisoned.
Photo courtesy National Archives*

On Monday April 13, Dad's friend, Mr. Uyeno, came with his large truck to carry us all, himself included, to the "Santa Anita Assembly Center." I did not have a purse so I carried an empty Crisco can in which I had my toothbrush, toothpaste, a couple of pencils and a small tablet to keep record of where we went and what we did. I remember I was wearing a pink long-sleeved blouse and blue pants.

It was raining that day. Mom said it was *"nameda ama,"* which means "rain tears" in Japanese.

When we reached our destination, we discovered that the "assembly center" was Santa Anita Racetrack in Arcadia, California. As we got off the bus, we saw several very tall guard towers. The entire track was surrounded by a barbed-wire fence, with about 200 soldiers with guns guarding the perimeter. We were only 15 miles or so from our home in Downey, but it already felt like we had been deposited into a cruel distant world.

We were searched to see if we had anything sharp or any cameras, both of which were prohibited. My father carried a small pocketknife that he used to clean his fingernails, but the authorities took it away.

Our family was assigned to live in a horse stall. The floor was dirt and there were three cots lined up head-to-head. We could smell the strong odor of horse manure and urine. We wondered if anyone had even tried to make the horse stalls habitable for humans. Our hearts sank.

My father said, "We are poor, but we have never lived

in a place like this." We felt powerless and very unhappy. My father said, "There's nothing we can do."

For five months, our family of six lived in this one-room, dirt-floor horse stall, wondering every day how long we would be forced to stay there. The partition separating our stall from the family next to us didn't go all the way to the ceiling, so there was no privacy. We could hear them and they could hear us. There was no kitchen, and terrible communal bathrooms that also had no partitions. Some families were assigned to live out by the grandstand of the racetrack. They had to sleep on mattresses filled with hay.

We learned to take it in stride, but it was hard. We eventually learned that there were 19,000 Japanese people being held at this racetrack, having been "evacuated" from all over California.

We didn't know it at the time, but this "assembly center," was the largest of its kind in the United States, one of 15 across the country. Today it is called what it really was: an internment camp. It was a place to confine people the government had no idea how to handle — even though the majority of us were American citizens.

Luggage of Japanese Americans deposited on the Santa Anita Racetrack; some families sitting with the only belongings they now owned. Photo by Russell Lee, courtesy United States Library of Congress

The government had created six mess halls to feed us, coded by colors, i.e. green, blue and orange. Each mess hall had three assigned times to eat each meal, 30 minutes apiece. For example, breakfast times were from 6 to 6:30 a.m. 6:30 to 7; and 7 to 7:30. The time we ate was according to the meal tickets we were given. That was apparently the only way the government could figure out how to feed nearly 20,000 prisoners daily. Fortunately, the food actually wasn't bad, but the noise level in the dishwashing area was ear-shattering.

We began to settle into a rhythm of tolerance. We became accustomed to the searchlights that swept the grounds nightly. And we found ways to keep clean, in spite of there being only 150 showers for the whole population.

We needed to do something to keep ourselves from thinking too much about where we were imprisoned and how long we would be stuck here — and to keep us from becoming angry and bitter. Dad raked the front of our horse stall to make it feel as livable as possible.

We were required to work in order to keep the camp running efficiently. Many of us worked in the mess halls as waiters, waitresses and dishwashers, and setting the long tables with place settings before each meal. I worked in the orange mess hall.

Mom worked as a dishwasher and cook's helper. I really do not remember what my youngest sister and brother did; they probably were looked after by young adults.

Many of the young girls had to make camouflage nets

for the military in a shop area set up on the grandstand of the track.

When the U.S. government decided it wanted more soldiers for the war effort, they invited young Japanese American men to join the Army. Amazingly, many of the men imprisoned at the racetrack volunteered. They became members of the 442nd Regimental Combat Team, whose ranks were filled completely by *Nisei* (first generation of Japanese born in America), except for the Caucasian officers. These young men sent most of their Army wages back to their parents, who were still locked up in internment camps.

The soldiers of the 442nd, combined with the 100th Infantry Battalion, received orders to fight in some of the bloodiest battles of the war in Europe. They became the most highly decorated units in U.S. military history at that time, earning more than 18,000 individual decorations for bravery.

Recently I learned that while we were living in that horse stall, my father signed up for the Fourth Registration of the Army draft, often referred to as the "old man's registration," for men who were between 45 and 64 years old. My father signed up to prove his loyalty to the United States. The whole situation was unjust, no matter how we looked at it.

To make life feel as normal as we possibly could, we also created some fun activities; for example, watching

REGISTRATION CARD—(Men born on or after April 28, 1877 and on or before February 16, 1897)

SERIAL NUMBER	1. NAME (Print)			ORDER NUMBER
U 1996	YOSHIGORO (First)	(NONE) (Middle)	KAWAGUCHI (Last)	

2 PLACE OF RESIDENCE (Print)

319 CONRAD ST.   DOWNEY   LOS ANGELES,   CALIF
(Number and street)   (Town, township, village, or city)   (County)   (State)

[THE PLACE OF RESIDENCE GIVEN ON THE LINE ABOVE WILL DETERMINE LOCAL BOARD JURISDICTION; LINE 2 OF REGISTRATION CERTIFICATE WILL BE IDENTICAL]

3. MAILING ADDRESS

SANTA ANITA ASSEMBLY CENTER   ARCADIA,   CALIF
[Mailing address if other than place indicated on Line 2. If same insert word same]

4. TELEPHONE	5. AGE IN YEARS	6. PLACE OF BIRTH
NONE	57	WAKAYAMA-KEN (Town or county)
	DATE OF BIRTH	
	MAY 28 1884	JAPAN
(Exchange) (Number)	(Mo.) (Day) (Yr.)	(State or country)

7. NAME AND ADDRESS OF PERSON WHO WILL ALWAYS KNOW YOUR ADDRESS

I. IKEGAMI   SANTA ANITA ASSEMBLY CENTER   ARCAD. CALIF.

8. EMPLOYER'S NAME AND ADDRESS

NONE

9. PLACE OF EMPLOYMENT OR BUSINESS

NONE

(Number and street or R.F.D. number)   (Town)   (County)   (State)

I AFFIRM THAT I HAVE VERIFIED ABOVE ANSWERS AND THAT THEY ARE TRUE.

D. S. S. Form 1 (Revised 4-1-42)   (over)   16—21630-2   (Registrant's signature)

My father's U.S. Army draft registration card that he signed
while our family was being forced to live in a horse stall.
Dad signed up to prove his loyalty to the United States.

sumo matches in the evening, and singing songs, sort of like today's karaoke. There were sewing classes, theater groups, a band and even a string quartet. There were also Boy Scout troops, a PTA and scores of softball teams.

In the evenings, some of us young people would sit in the grandstand and watch the trains going by on the tracks outside our jail. We wondered what each one was carrying: troops, war supplies or food? The outside world seemed so near as the trains rode past . . . until the reality of our forced confinement crept back into our minds.

I really do not know how we lived through all this in the face of so much uncertainty. We were safe in the moment, but we couldn't help wondering, "What will become of us?"

Life outside the "assembly center" continued on without us. In the month after we were "evacuated," neighbors came to pick all the produce on the farm that had ripened in our absence. I don't believe the farm owners got compensated for that at all.

Our neighbor who had agreed to look after our car and my sewing machine came to visit us at the horse stall a couple times. During one visit, he told us that he had sold the sewing machine for $25 and our 1930 Ford for $100. My father was happy about that, so I assume Dad understood that we might be here for a long time.

Ironically, the thing I missed the most while imprisoned in the horse stall was working on the farm. It had been hard work, but we had always been free.

As the months passed, we learned we were going to be released. But then a rumor started that we weren't really going to be free. Instead, we were going to be shipped to another internment camp where we would be imprisoned once more.

We read in the camp's newspaper, which was published by internees, and heard from our friends, that barracks were being built for us somewhere in the desert, with wooded areas being cleared to create additional space.

We were so worried, especially since my parents were getting old. My father was already 66, and had spent his whole life doing physical labor.

We heard the government had arranged passage on two ships for anyone who wanted to be repatriated to Japan. A Swedish cruise line had agreed to exchange diplomats, women, children and prisoners between the United States and Japan. By the war's end, the two ships had made a combined 33 voyages, sailing through mine- and submarine-riddled oceans with all their lights on, to avoid being mistaken for a battleship.

I didn't know it at the time, but my father had signed our family name to be on the second ship, the MV Gripsholm. I don't know why we didn't get on that ship, but I was told it didn't come.

Whatever the reason, I'm happy we weren't on that ship. Otherwise, who knows? We may have all been killed by one of the atomic bombs the United States military dropped on Japan.

Chapter 8
Rohwer Internment Camp: Gaman

After five months living in that horse stall, our family was required to pack up again, putting our meager belongings into one suitcase apiece. We, along with at least 10,000 other Japanese people who had been held at Santa Anita Racetrack, were loaded onto trains. We had no idea where we were being taken, only that we were no closer to being free than we had been for the prior five months.

While on the train, we were ordered to keep the blinds down over our windows. I don't know if this was so we could not see the outside world that we were no longer part of, or if it was to protect us from people who would not understand that the Japanese faces looking out were Americans, and not the enemy. Nevertheless, I peeked out of my window.

As we passed the Southern California towns of Colton and Beaumont, I saw nothing but rolling hills, and I knew we were heading east. We passed date farms in Indio, then miles and miles of desert through Coachella Valley. Just before sundown, the desert hills turned purple in the waning light. In the deserts of Arizona, I saw Yucca trees and cactus for miles. While going through New Mexico, there was sagebrush as far as my eyes could see.

On the second day, as we passed through Texas and several other states, I saw hoboes living in train boxcars. I saw cotton fields after cotton fields, miles and miles worth. Small shacks dotted the landscape, and I assumed that's where the hired farmhands lived. The scenes made me yearn for the simpler years of my childhood. We had worked long days doing manual labor on the farm, but at least we had our freedom.

Between sneaking peeks out the window and sleeping on the seats, I ate meals in the dining car with my family where, thankfully, the food was pretty good. Under dramatically different circumstances, I might have enjoyed this journey. But we had no idea what would become of us.

After four days and three nights, transferring trains several times, we arrived at our destination of Rohwer, Arkansas at 4:30 p.m. on September 24, 1942, feeling dusty, dirty and ragged.

The first thing we saw was barbed-wire fences and high watchtowers, with soldiers aiming rifles at endless rows of barracks. The sign outside euphemistically called it "Rohwer Relocation Center."

I wondered, "What kind of place is this?" We soon learned it was another, more permanent, internment camp for U.S. residents of Japanese ancestry, with 500 acres of tar-papered barracks hastily built to hold 8,000 people.

Rohwer was one of 10 similar "concentration camps," as we came to call them, across the nation. Our family was only six of 120,000 Japanese Americans in the same plight. I don't know if that made us feel better or worse.

Our new "home" was a one-room corner barrack, number 21-2F, that had three canvas cots lined up head-to-head. All six of us living in one room again. Thank goodness when we arrived, we had no idea we would spend the next two years in this God-forsaken place.

There is a word in the Japanese language that describes what our mindset became. *Gaman*: enduring the seemingly unbearable with patience and dignity.

To someone unacquainted with the concept of *gaman*, it probably appeared that Japanese-Americans who were sent to internment camps during World War II were submissive, too obedient for their own good or simply very docile.

In reality, our understanding of *gaman* is to remain strong in the face of adversity, regardless of how much suffering we feel.

Oh, the Japanese people, we were very accepting at that time. But I know stories of a few Japanese people who became terribly angry and embittered by the entire experience. They allowed it to affect them for the rest of their lives, and by association, their children's lives.

I understand why they were angry. My family and I experienced the same hardships. Our choice was to respond more quietly, while appreciating whatever good we could find — or create — in terrible situations. I believe that our positive outlook enabled us to endure the years we were wrongly imprisoned, and once we were released, to be happy during the rest of our lives.

Chapter 9
Life Behind Barbed Wire

After overcoming our initial shock, our family set about making the best of our circumstances while living behind barbed wire.

The only furniture in our room besides the cots was a wood-burning pot-bellied stove that we were grateful to have when the weather turned cold and it began snowing. Over time, my father gathered several small boxes for us to store the very few clothes we had been able to bring with us. He also made some rudimentary furniture using empty fruit crates, like a table where we ironed our clothes.

As we had experienced while living at Santa Anita Racetrack, the shower room was communal, shared with many people. We wore *getas*, traditional Japanese sandals with elevated wooden soles, to avoid coming in contact with germs on our feet.

The lack of privacy everywhere — in the one room our family lived in, the bathrooms and the shower room — was something we simply had to get accustomed to. We had no choice.

We were required to work in this camp, too. Father worked in the mess hall as kitchen helper and Mom was a dishwasher. I worked in the recreation hall as a seamstress and made coveralls for the internees who were allowed out of the camp daily to work on farms in the surrounding areas.

The government paid us between $12 and $15 per month, averaging 70 cents per day. In contrast, our friends in the world outside earned about $6 per day. With our tiny wages, we had to purchase all our own clothing, shoes and other necessities like soap, shampoo and toothpaste.

In our spare time, we made many craft items. Every time there was a funeral, a lot of us ladies got together and made flowers from colored paper. We did what we could to bring life to such somber events, so very important to our souls during this confinement.

Mom became adept with a pocketknife, making beautiful wood carvings out of the cone-shaped growths on the roots of the cypress trees that grew in the area. I wish I had kept some of the lovely things she carved.

One of the few blessings of our time in Arkansas is that I was able to begin doing needlework again. Back on the farm on rainy days, we three sisters would sit around a table and draw a picture of an apple or an orange or a flower. My mother would give us colored threads to stitch our designs.

When we were confined at the Santa Anita Racetrack, I didn't have my beloved needlework as my creative outlet. After we were relocated to Arkansas, I was able to start sewing again. I taught myself all kinds of techniques: appliqué, cross-stitch, crewel, embroidery. I also made

View of barracks at Rohwer Relocation Center where our family of six lived in one room for two years. The wooden walkway was how we crossed over the drainage ditch that surrounded each block.
Photographer: Gretchen Van Tassel, courtesy National Archives

stuffed toys of all kinds, beaded flowers, fabric flowers, lace cloths and more. It was such a blessing to be able to make beautiful things to help make our stark living conditions bearable. I continued my needlework for decades after we became free again.

We purchased all our supplies from the Sears, Roebuck and Co. and Montgomery Ward catalogs, though Sears was more popular. It was amazing that those department stores delivered to this government-run prison. They helped us keep our worries at bay while we occupied our hands and minds. I hope they made a fortune!

The food at Rohwer was very good, compared to Santa Anita. We ate a lot of shrimp, probably thanks to how close the camp was to the Mississippi River. The government may even have had shrimp shipped up from the Gulf of Mexico for us. We also ate a lot of dried fruits, as there were many farms surrounding the camp, and rice, thanks to nearby rice growers.

Some people in the camp even had small vegetable gardens, but by then, my parents felt too old to farm anymore.

In hindsight, it seems as though the Rohwer camp was more relaxed than some of the other internment camps across the country. There was church service on Sunday; there was a hospital. You could learn to read and write Japanese. There were regular classes for school-age children. There was even a post office and a library. They really tried to take good care of us.

We made many new friends while living this communal life. We all had in common similar hardships and therefore understood each other. Everybody got along well with each other.

Every day took a long time to pass because it was so hard to keep busy and we still didn't know how long we would be incarcerated. But somehow we always knew we would be all right.

Classes were taught to school-age children at Rohwer Relocation Center in Arkansas to make our incarceration seem somewhat normal. In this picture, second graders sit in a "classroom" that makes the two-room schoolhouse I attended as a child seem luxurious. Photographer Tom Parker. Courtesy National Archives

Chapter 10
Rejoining America

Two years passed with us confined in this Arkansas "relocation camp," while the world continued outside of our guarded, barbed-wire borders.

Finally the U.S. government decided to allow some of us to rejoin America, even though the war was not over yet. In order to be allowed out, we had to provide three letters of recommendation from people outside the camp, people to whom we were not related. The irony of that was not lost on us. Most of our friends were still imprisoned, too.

We were tremendously fortunate that my father had worked so many years for Mr. Hiram Johnson, who had now become a United States senator. Two of our family's three letters of recommendation came from his family. Of all the employers Dad could have found when he came to America, what good fortune! Thanks to Mr. Johnson, we were some of the first internees to leave Rohwer.

Shortly before we left, camp authorities provided us each with $26. I wondered how in the world we were going to pay rent and buy food until we all found work with only $26 apiece! My father was 67 years old, and though my mother was much younger at 45, neither was excited to start their working lives all over again. But what choice did we have? My parents thought about returning to Japan, but quickly decided against that idea, preferring to stay close to us.

Just as we were preparing to leave the camp, good fortune smiled on us again. A friend we had made in Rohwer when he had lived in the barracks across from us, Mr. Yoshihara, had been freed shortly before we were. He wrote us a letter that he was working on a farm in Almont, Michigan, and invited us to help him. My parents decided to take a chance. My father said he was curious to see what was planted on the farm.

Our family of six packed our few belongings and left Rohwer on the Southern Pacific train. At that time, seating on the train was still segregated: we all sat in the front and there was a large blind pulled behind us to separate the white people from the blacks. We thought that was just terrible. After we, as Japanese Americans, had been removed from society for two-and-a-half years, now we were being allowed to sit in front of other U.S. citizens as if we were better than they were. It was bizarre.

When we reached our destination, the Yoshiharas came to pick us up and showed us the farm. It was quite large, about 50 acres, planted mostly in wax beans and cauliflower, with a wooded forest on part of the acreage.

The farmworkers' house we stayed in was a tumble-down shack with three beds lined up head-to-head. My sister Yoneko and I shared a bed, as did my sister

Yoshino and my brother.

There was a small kitchen, no refrigerator, and we shared a bathroom and *furo* with the Yoshiharas. There was an outdoor faucet with a small table and pan, over which we washed our faces in cold water and brushed our teeth. When we were finished, we threw the water in the yard.

When the wind blew from the north, and when it snowed in winter, the kitchen pipe would freeze. Dad tied a light bulb to the pipe to keep the water from freezing.

Our living conditions were considerably more primitive than the first shack we had lived in on the farm back in Downey, California. But our family was still together, and for the first time in two-and-a-half years, we were free.

After several months, my parents realized it was too difficult for them to work on a farm at their ages. Dad asked me to contact the War Relocation Authority (a government agency) to find out if they could help find an easier place for them to live and work. The WRA man, Mr. Marsa, took my father and me to another farm to see if it would be any easier, but my father said it was time for him to do different work.

Mr. Marsa found jobs for my parents, my sister Yoshino, and brother Yoshio, at Holly's Restaurant in South Haven, Michigan. My father worked as the janitor, my mother worked in the kitchen, and my sister and brother waited tables.

It was at Holly's where Yoshino was given the English

name of Bernice, and Yoshio was given the name Frank. I don't know why, probably to save the restaurant owners from outcry among local residents who still harbored anti-Japanese sentiment.

My brother Frank (Yoshio) and my father while working at Holly's Restaurant in South Haven, Michigan. Frank was a cook and my father worked as a janitor.

My parents worked at Holly's for five years. Frank completed his senior year of high school and received his diploma. Bernice didn't seem to mind her new name, but she did not like being a waitress, so she found work at an ammunition factory. I always wondered if that was really better.

Chapter 11
Becoming Susan

My sister Yoneko and I were spared having to work more than several months on the farm thanks to the Nakashimas, a family we became good friends with while living in adjoining horse stalls at the Santa Anita Racetrack.

The Nakashima's son and daughter had been working in the very upscale area of Bloomfield Hills, Michigan, at a restaurant named the Devon Gables Tea Room. Their son had been called back into the military, and their daughter, a waitress, was getting married. When the family came to see us on the farm in Almont, they said their boss asked if they would find someone to take their places at the restaurant. The Nakashimas asked if Yoneko and I were interested.

We didn't want to be separated from our family, but my father said that at our ages, the farm was no place for us girls. Thank goodness he encouraged us. Working at Devon Gables changed my life.

The Devon Gables Tea Room was an elegant restaurant that served lunch and dinner. The building was beautiful English-style architecture. The entrance to the dining hall was always decorated for the changing seasons. Tables were set with pretty white lace doilies that had been hand-made by a blind girl.

There were several nice dining rooms. One was called the Nantucket Room, decorated in sea ornaments with tables and chairs to match, all colored grayish-bluish to match the ocean. In the main dining room was a beautiful yellow canary in a cage that would sing while people were dining. One special girl took care of the canary, feeding and covering the cage at night.

Postcard of Devon Gables Tea Room in Bloomfield Hills, Michigan.

We didn't know it at the time, but one Michigan news-paper named Devon Gables "one of America's most distin-guished and distinctive tea rooms."

When my sister and I arrived at Devon Gables, everything was so new to us, since we had never had any contact with the outside world, beyond going to school and working on the farm. We had never imagined ourselves working in such beautiful surroundings and with such nice people. We were so happy.

Bloomfield Hills was a very influential community located about 18 miles outside Detroit. As a waitress, I served a lot of doctors, teachers, the higher-class people. My sister and I learned that those people were very courteous. We saw the way they dressed and listened to how they spoke to their guests who joined them for a meal. We learned how to use a fork and knife, how to eat a salad. Until then, all we had known was farm life, where all six of us would sit around a round table and we'd grab whatever we needed out of the big pot, and eat with our chopsticks.

We made good friends with some of the people who came to Devon Gables. They invited us to their homes to eat dinner. We hadn't known what it was like to be invited by Caucasian people. Oh, we just enjoyed meeting so many nice people.

When I began working at Devon Gables, I was a very shy girl. I soon told myself, "I can't be bashful to wait on people," so I had to change. I'm glad I did.

When I started working at Devon Gables, my name was Yoshiko. The owner, a beautiful platinum blonde woman named Laura Harvey, gave me the name Susan, and she gave my sister, Yoneko, the name Frances. I think she gave us English names because when she started hiring Japanese workers from the relocation camps, she received many threatening letters.

One year after the war ended, there was still a lot of anti-Japanese sentiment in the United States. A perfect example was in a very flattering article about Devon Gables in the The Detroit News, a major Michigan newspaper, touting our excellent service:

> *In short, they are perfect waitresses. But you'd better stay away from the place unless you can stand a surprise. These paragons are not of our own superior race, but are relocated Japanese.*

Maybe it was a blessing that we got our English names.

At first, we still called our family members by our Japanese names. But in a short time, we got used to our English names. My father said, "This is America. We should use our English names."

Now we use only our English names. My sisters and brother call me Susan, but they also like to call me Susie and Susie Q. I love the name Susan.

We were paid 50 cents per hour for waitressing and we got to keep our tips. On Saturdays and Sundays, our tips were very good. My sister also typed the dinner menu as it changed according to the fresh fruits, vegetables, meats and fish that were being served each night.

Laura provided room and board to everyone who worked at Devon Gables. Frances and I shared a double bed in the attic of the restaurant. Our bedroom was very comfortable, with a nightstand, a lamp, and I had bought a small plastic clock with an alarm so we could get up at 6 a.m.

We shared this room with another lady named Viola, who worked as a cook. Above the attic was one more room lived in by a girl named Betty. On the other side of the building lived a Japanese couple; the husband cleaned the chickens for the restaurant's famous chicken croquettes and chicken pies; the wife was a waitress. There was one bathroom shared by everyone who lived on the west side of the building, and another for those on the east side of the building.

Laura was very particular how we dressed. We had to be very neat. White shoes, clean aprons, washed, starched and neatly pressed. We had to wear hairnets. Our shoes and shoelaces needed to be white. When we came down for breakfast at 7:30 every morning, we had to be dressed nicely, and be ready to work immediately after breakfast.

At the end of each day, after the restaurant closed at 8:30 p.m., we cleaned everything, including stretching the lace doilies on a special stretcher. We finally got to our rooms to take our shoes off at 10 p.m. They were long days, but my sister and I thought nothing of it. It was so much easier than working on a farm. In fact, we enjoyed it so much, we couldn't wait to get up the next morning to start work.

I worked at Devon Gables Tea Room for three-and-a-half years. My sister Frances worked there for six years. What great experiences I had working there! I learned things I would never have learned in school. It was such a different world than any I had been exposed to on the farm, and a far cry from any life I had imagined for myself while we were imprisoned in a horse stall and in a one-room barrack in Rohwer, Arkansas.

My sister Frances, right, and me
all dressed up to go shopping in Detroit.
That's Laura's dog at our feet.

Chapter 12
Mr. Tom T. Matsumoto

One December while my sister and I were working at Devon Gables, Laura gave us two weeks off. Frances said, "We have enough money saved to go to Chicago." So off we went to visit a girlfriend who lived there.

During our visit, our girlfriend asked us, "Do you want to meet some boys from Hawaii?" I said, "Sure, why not?"

That's how I met Tom. He was a young Japanese American man, born on the island of Kauai, who had been visiting some of his Hawaii-born friends in an apartment at the opposite side of the building where we were staying. All of them had recently completed their wartime service with the U.S. Army.

I didn't know it yet, but Tom would become my husband. At that time, getting married was the last thing I wanted.

Years earlier, when I had been attending the Parisian School of Fashion Arts in Los Angeles, I read a newspaper story about a Japanese woman who had worked for a

Caucasian movie star. When the movie star passed away, she left her employee $10,000! In those days, $10,000 was a lot of money. I thought, "Well, forget about boyfriends. I'll work for the Hollywood movie stars."

So here I was, working at Devon Gables Tea Room and, for the first time in my life, making my own way in the world. I wasn't looking for a boyfriend. I didn't care about getting married. I was independent. I had made up my mind.

Well, Tom and I got to be friends, and when he returned home to California where he lived, we kept in contact for awhile. Then we lost touch and I forgot all about him. A co-worker of mine at Devon Gables, who had been a reporter for a Japanese language newspaper before he was interned, offered to introduce me to a Japanese dentist, but that never materialized.

Then one day Tom came to visit me at Devon Gables. I must have told him where I worked, though I don't recall that conversation. I assume he filed it away in his memory for the next time he visited his buddies in Chicago. I thought, "He's a pretty good guy." But I was still uninterested in anything formal. I was more focused on experiencing and enjoying my new life.

After Tom returned to California again, he started sending me cards and candies for Valentine's Day, Easter and Christmas, too, and we began keeping in touch by writing letters. This was long before computers were household items, of course.

Through our correspondence, I learned that Tom had been born in 1916 in the tiny town of Kekaha on the sleepy west side of Kauai, one of the smaller Hawaiian islands. Remember how after Pearl Harbor was bombed, I thought it would be fascinating to meet someone from Hawaii? Well, here he was. Isn't that interesting?

Tom had only attended grammar school, and as a teenager, he worked for Kekaha Sugar Plantation as a sugar cane carrier. His father worked in the cane fields, too, and his mother did laundry for the plantation.

Tom realized he wanted to do something more interesting with his life, and wanted to see more of the world than a sugar plantation. So at age 19, with $50 in his pocket, he took a Matson ship from Hawaii to Los Angeles, an arduous five-day journey in those days, especially traveling in steerage, where people who could only afford the least expensive tickets had to ride.

When he arrived in Los Angeles, reality set in. He knew no one in the city and felt very far away from his small island where everyone knew everyone. He sat down and cried.

He quickly regrouped and began taking odd jobs,

like working for the United Parcel Service and cleaning a beauty shop after it closed for the day. He also sold produce at the 9th Street Market, the same place where the produce my parents grew while working for the Ikegamis in Downey used to be sold. How about that?

Soon he met a few other young men from Hawaii, and together they rented an apartment. He attended an auto mechanic school and got his mechanic's license. He was inducted into the U.S. Army in 1941.

Tom told me that while he was in the military, he was stationed primarily at Fort Sam Houston in San Antonio, Texas, processing recruits. Other than this, he never said a word about his time in the Army.

During his time in the military, Tom visited some Japanese friends at several of the internment camps, so he had a feeling for what my family and I had been through for two-and-a-half years, without me having to explain much to him.

After serving for four years and four months, Tom was discharged from the Army. Shortly after that, he had come to Chicago to visit his friends — and met me. Although I had not thought about getting married, I had always felt more comfortable with him than with anyone else, besides my family, of course. And though I didn't know it yet, marrying him was going to change my life.

By this time I was 26 years old, and my mother often reminded me that I was getting old. She kept saying, "If you found a nice one, you better get married."

Finally, once when I was visiting my parents in South Haven, Michigan, Tom called me to say he was going to come visit from California to see my parents, but he did not tell me why. He asked for me to please reserve a hotel room for him. I think he stayed for about two days, and in that time, he asked my parents in broken Japanese if he could marry me. I thought that was so nice of him, because my mother still couldn't understand English too well.

We were married on May 3, 1947, by a Zen Buddhist priest at the YMCA in Chicago. Our reception was at the Wisteria restaurant. My family all came via taxi from Michigan. It was a small gathering, about 35 friends attended. Tom's family was far away on the Hawaiian island of Kauai.

Neither of our parents had much money, so I paid for all my wedding expenses. I did not want to wear a wedding gown. I was just a simple girl. I didn't like to wear fancy dresses. Instead, I picked out a beautiful teal blue two-piece suit, a lovely pink hat and teal blue earrings to match my suit.

After we were married, Tom and I wanted to live in Chicago. My family was so sad to see me leave Michigan; they wanted me to stay near them. But I knew it was time to make a new life with my husband.

Our wedding day, May 3, 1947.

Chapter 13
On Our Own

To tell you the truth, Tom was different from any other Japanese boy I had ever known. He was so kind, and he was always joking around. There was a commercial on television for a drink named Hawaiian Punch in which a man would say, "How'd you like a nice Hawaiian punch?" Then he would hand another person a can of the fruity juice. Tom loved that ad. He would jokingly make a fist and say, "You want a Hawaiian punch?" That was one of his favorite jokes.

I was always good at breaking things around our home. I don't remember how I did it but I broke one of our favorite lamps. I felt so bad, but Tom never made a big fuss about it. He said to me, "Even us, you and me, we are not going to last forever either."

One day, I was washing one of my favorite flower vases that a good friend had given me, and I broke it. Tom said, "Some things are made to be broken. You can always buy a new one, and we get to support the companies who make the things you break."

I guess I balanced out my habit of breaking things with my habit of keeping clothing items forever. Tom used to say, "You're always darning your socks. Get rid of those things and get some new ones!" I don't know why I became so frugal, maybe because of my upbringing on the farm, when money was so tight, or from having so little in the years my family lived in the internment camps. I'm still that way today, and it has always paid off.

When we first got married, there were almost no vacancies for apartments in Chicago, so we took what we could get. We found a one-room apartment on the fourth floor of a large brick building named LaSalle Mansion. The owner was a Japanese man who had cut up his house into multiple apartments. I don't know why he did that. Maybe he had owned this nice home before World War II and had been imprisoned in internment camps, like our family had been. Maybe it was the only way he could still afford to keep his property.

Whatever the reason, our apartment in this mansion cost only $8 per week. It was less than optimal, but it was all we could find. We had to share a community bathroom with other people on the same floor, which I did not like. It was too reminiscent of my years in the camps, but at least now I knew it was only temporary. We also shared the phone on the third floor with all the other tenants.

The apartment had no cooking equipment, so we bought a one-burner electric stove. Our room was so tiny, we had to place the burner on top of our two green suitcases. To make dinner, we had to cook the rice first, then the rest of the meal separately.

We didn't have a refrigerator, but thankfully there was a store across the street, where every day I bought eight slices of lunchmeat or chicken to make our lunches for work, a couple of bananas or apples, and a small bag of potato chips. When we bought eggs, we stored them in the coolest part of the room. It was hard climbing up to the fourth floor every time we returned home, but we were younger in those days so it was not too bad.

Eventually a larger apartment on the third floor of this building opened up, and we were happy to take it. I think much of our new living quarters had once been a very large bathroom in the mansion, because our kitchen sink was quite small and bathroom size. But we finally had enough space for a two-burner stove. It was nice cooking a complete meal at once, and now that we had a small gas refrigerator, we could save our leftovers. We also had a window, which was nice during the cold winter days, when I could leave fruit out on the windowsill and not crowd our little refrigerator. We even had a very little dining room. It was definitely a step up.

After six years working at the Devon Gables Tea Room, my sister, Frances, decided to move to Chicago to be near me. My sister, Bernice, joined her, and together they moved into the apartment next door to Tom's and mine in the mansion. It was nice having them close to us, and sharing the bathroom with my sisters was much more comfortable than sharing it with strangers.

My sisters had a wooden icebox. That's what people used if they didn't have a refrigerator. You would put a block of ice at the top of this large wooden box, and a large pan in the bottom caught the water as the ice melted. The temperature of the ice kept the food cold. When my sisters needed more ice, they displayed their "ICE" sign in our window, to alert the ice delivery man, who made his deliveries using a cart pulled by a horse.

Soon my parents also moved to Chicago to be closer to us. Mom and Dad both found work at the Edgewater Beach Hotel, Mom as a maid and Dad cleaning the hotel.

It felt natural for our family to be near each other again. We celebrated holidays together. In fact, Dad had adjusted to America so much, that he no longer liked too much Japanese food. He had learned to eat steak and boy, oh boy, he loved it until his dying day. On New Year's Day, we normally celebrated in traditional Japanese style, but one of my sisters would cook our father a juicy steak and he would be so happy.

After eight years living in apartments in LaSalle Mansion, Tom and I had saved up enough money to buy a nice two-story brick house of our own on Larabee Street in Chicago. We rented out the first floor and kept the basement and second floor to ourselves. Our new home had everything we wanted: privacy, lots of extra space, and all the appliances we could imagine. For the first time, we had our own bathroom, complete with a four-legged tub. The kitchen had a huge pantry with a window. We had a full-size gas stove to cook to our heart's content, and we had air conditioning to keep us cool in the hot summer months.

My parents in South Haven, Michigan in the mid-1940s.

In the winters, I used to get up at 5 a.m. to shovel the snow out front and salt the driveway to melt the snow. We were young at that time, so we did not mind the cold, sleet and snow too much. Besides, it was a pleasure to take care of our very own home.

We loved living in Chicago. There was a bakery near our home, and also a café that made the best tamales wrapped in corn husks. When Tom and I had days off from

work, we enjoyed walking along Lakeshore Drive, which ran along Lake Michigan, up to Grant Park and The Loop, which was Chicago's shopping district. We would buy a bag of peanuts and casually walk back home eating our nuts. We went to plays, and many a time the theaters in Chicago would have an orchestra perform before the show started.

Growing up on a farm, then being imprisoned for two-and-a-half years, I'm not sure I ever really thought about what my life might be like, once I was out on my own. Now I was living a life better than I could have ever imagined.

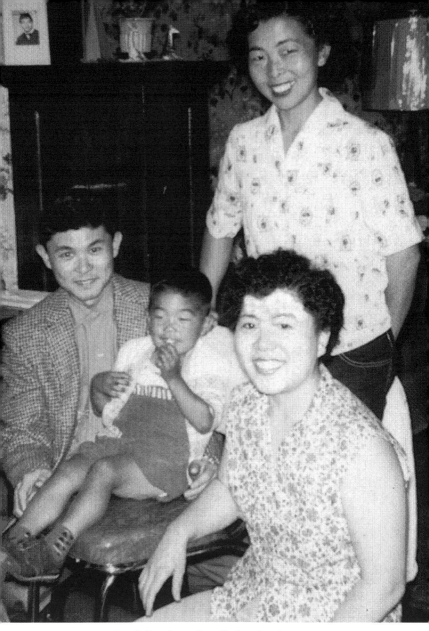

Frank, Bernice and me (in front) with
Bernice's son Stanley, in Chicago.

Chapter 14
Hawaiian Mailman in Chicago

Tom worked at the Mohr Lino-Saw factory, and in the evenings, attended Crane Technical High School to get his high school diploma. Once he graduated, he started working at the post office during the Christmas holidays, and studied to take the exam to join the U.S. Postal Service as a mail carrier.

At the time, we were still living in our first small apartment in that four-story mansion. Whenever Tom was studying, he constantly heard what sounded like a little child upstairs jumping off the bed and making so much noise that he was not able to concentrate. One day he went upstairs to ask them if they could help their little one be a bit quieter. Well, Tom was so friendly that in no time, they were all getting along famously. And when we learned that this young couple was originally from Honolulu, Hawaii, and they found out that Tom was from Kauai, we all became good friends. What a small world it is.

Tom passed his postal service exam! I was so proud of him, a boy with only a grammar school education, finding a way to advance himself for our future.

Tom loved everyone on his mail delivery route, and he loved surprising them with gifts. I used to do needlework to keep me busy during winter months, making a lot of kitchen towels, many with the old pancake syrup character, Aunt Jemima, on them. Whatever I made, Tom gave away to his patrons at Christmas, and his customers loved them. The patrons would invite us out for dinner. The people in Chicago were so nice! Tom just loved people — and dogs.

Every day Tom used to take three cookies to work in his pocket. At first I thought maybe he was getting together with someone for coffee. Then one day I discovered that he delivered mail to a gas station where the owner had three dogs. Every day he gave a cookie to each of the dogs while on his mail route.

The children on Tom's route all loved him, too. There was one home where, every time the woman of the house opened her door to receive the mail, her little boy would sneak around her, run to Tom's three-wheeled mail truck, and perch himself in the driver's seat. With his small hands on the steering wheel, the boy would make what he thought were noises of a motor starting: "Hmmm, hmmm." Tom would let him sit there for a moment, then say, "I have to go back to work delivering mail now, so you have to go back to your mother." Every time, the boy would say, "Mr. Mailman, just let me stay here for a little while longer." When Tom finally drove away, the little boy always ran behind the truck, following Tom to the next corner.

In the 20 years we lived in Chicago, mail was delivered

on Christmas Day. Oh my goodness, Tom's patrons were so happy. You should have seen all the monetary gifts he received. His jacket and pants pockets would be jammed full!

Tom always enjoyed being a mailman, especially when the weather was warm. But every year when winter came, bringing sleet, snow and freezing cold temperatures, he talked about going home to Hawaii. When spring came again and the snow began to melt, he remembered how much he enjoyed Chicago, and all the customers on his route.

Chapter 15
Rachel

Three years after Tom and I got married, I knew something was wrong with me. I told him, "I don't feel right." The doctor said I had a tumor on my uterus and told me that I would never be able to have any children. I cried. I wanted to have children with Tom. He loved children so much. I was 28 years old.

Tom said he saw the tumor after the doctor removed it, and it was the size of a golf ball. After it was removed, I had thousands and thousands of radiation units to be sure nothing like that ever came back again.

Several years later, Tom spotted a cute little Japanese girl at the Children's Home & Aid Society, a foster care and adoption facility where he used to deliver mail.

After a year or so of working with social workers, we adopted Rachel in 1954. Every day I tried to teach her how to say her name, but she had a hard time learning because

it was different than the name she was given before we adopted her. Finally she learned that her name was Rachel Matsumoto.

Several months after we brought her home, it was time to send her to kindergarten. Tom's mail route included Rachel's school. The teacher used to tell Rachel, "Your father is delivering the mail now. Go and say hello to him." They both enjoyed that.

Rachel was a smart girl, but on her first report card from school, her teacher had written, "She is a little bossy."

As a little girl, Rachel loved the outdoors. One day she told Tom, "Dad, I want a bicycle."

We didn't know how we were going to afford a bike. Tom and I were having a difficult time paying our mortgage. I wasn't working at the time so that I could make a nice home for all of us.

Fortunately, Tom heard that the police department was auctioning off bicycles that had been stolen and recovered from the thieves. On the appointed Saturday, Tom attended the auction. He was outbid on every bike — until the very last one. It was not in great shape, but for $8 Tom was the winning bidder.

Rachel was waiting at home with me, looking out the window. When she spotted him, she shouted, "Mom, here comes Dad. I see a bicycle sticking out of the trunk of his car!" She was so happy!

She could not ride the bike for awhile, for all the repairs it needed. Gradually Tom got that bicycle into good shape, even adding a basket on the front, as our daughter had requested.

After Rachel started riding her good-as-new bicycle around town, all her friends began coming over to ask Tom to fix their bikes! For awhile Tom was busy pumping air and doing minor repairs on lots of little girls' bicycles.

It was all worth it when we watched Rachel put on her small straw hat and ride her bike with friends on sunny days. We were both so pleased to be able to provide for our little girl an easier childhood than either Tom or I had experienced.

I have snapshots in my mind of moments in Rachel's life:

For some years, Rachel sang in the choir — and always volunteered, "My mother will wash and clean the choir robes."

As she got older, we loved taking her and her girl-friend ice skating at the park in winters, while Tom and I waited in the car.

In the evenings, Rachel and I would watch from our third floor apartment window and wave at Tom as he picked up mail from the blue mailbox on the corner across the street from us, when he was working the night shift. Rachel was so happy to see him!

When she came of age, Tom taught our daughter how to drive.

When Rachel got married, we were able to pay for half of her wedding.

Today our daughter has blessed us with three grandchildren. We enjoyed growing up with Rachel.

Chapter 16
All in a Day's Work

When Tom and I got married, neither one of us had much money nor marketable skills, so we agreed not to be fussy, and to take any kind of jobs we could find. He was fortunate to land work as a mailman, and he loved it.

I, on the other hand, worked in eight different places while we lived in Chicago. I learned something from each one of them.

I worked in a factory making gloves for firemen.

At the same time, I had a part-time job making beautiful artificial geraniums and other flowers. I would walk two blocks from our apartment to the business, Empire Arts, pick up the materials and bring them home to work on in the evenings. Some nights Tom helped me wrap green paper around the wire stems. I often imagined those flowers being displayed in lovely vases in people's homes.

After the glove factory, I worked at Feldman's Hat Company, making straw hats, and doing spring and summer piecework. Feldman's had a beautiful showroom where buyers came from all over the United States to purchase for their own stores. I was the only Japanese person working there at that time.

I did a lot of sewing headbands and sweatbands for the inside of hats. I was paid $2 an hour. (I think Tom was making only 75 cents an hour at the post office in those days.) At $2 an hour, I didn't want to waste a minute so I worked very fast. In fact, two black women who worked there were so nice to me. They said, "Susan, don't bother getting up. We will bring pieces to you." I left Feldman's Hat Company after I had worked myself up in the factory far enough that there was nothing left for me to learn.

Tom used to deliver mail to McCall's Patterns and got me a part-time job there. Well, I was familiar with this company, having been so fond of sewing clothing for most of my life. But there wasn't much for me to learn there, simply picking patterns off shelves that people ordered so they could be shipped to customers. I wanted to learn how to work the machine that printed addresses on shipping envelopes, but the woman who had that job showed no signs of leaving anytime soon.

I found a part-time job sewing plastic raincoats. I stayed at that job only six weeks. They paid me only once a month, which was challenging for us. The pay wasn't that good anyway, so I quit.

One of my two favorite places I worked in Chicago was at Leeds Sweete, where I worked for seven years. I learned to bake plastic molds for hobbyists and for kits for Boy Scouts, how to do silk screening, and I also packed orders that people placed for crayons. I really enjoyed what I was doing there. My pay was 75 cents an hour.

For some reason, the owner of Leeds Sweete hired

only Japanese people. Most of them could not speak English well, but they did the jobs they were taught, and were good, fast and reliable.

One day I learned that the business next door, Stereo Optical, was taking over the whole building and they needed one more person, so I began working for them.

I worked at Leeds Sweete for seven years baking plastic molds for hobbyists. I also learned how to do silk screening while I worked there.

Stereo Optical was a small company, maybe only 11 people. I did the same thing all day, assembling part of eyeglasses. I thought, "What an easy job!" I was paid $1.75 an hour.

Chris Lewis, the owner of Stereo Optical, was a great boss. I really enjoyed working for him, and never had another boss like him, before or since. He told me I was the first Japanese lady he had ever hired. He told me, "I never knew Japanese people were such good workers."

For a boss, Chris was very social with us employees, something I had never experienced before. After lunchtime, he loved to play the card game Rummy with us. Fortunately, Tom had taught me how to play Rummy some years earlier. When it was time to go back to work, Chris always said, "Let's play another hand."

Some days, Tom came to pick me up after work.

When I would go out to the car, guess what? Chris would be sitting in our car talking with Tom! I had never seen a boss like that.

One day I learned that some of the other employees at Stereo Optical were receiving overtime pay. I was not afraid of anything anymore in those days, so I went knocking at Chris's door. I asked him, "Chris, why is it the other girls are all getting extra pay? I'd like to have overtime pay, too." He gave it to me.

When I left the company, Chris gave me a Hawaiian-style farewell party. In hindsight, I find that very interesting. How could he have known that some years later, Tom and I would make our home in Hawaii?

Chapter 17
Learning to Drive #1

Ever since I first met Tom, he wanted to teach me how to drive. But I wasn't interested at all.

I said, "What on Earth do I have to learn to drive for? Here in Chicago we have the El (elevated trains), the subway, the bus and the trolley."

For awhile, Tom was determined. I was apparently not a very good student. Our driving lessons were the only times my very happy husband had any degree of a sour disposition.

He tried and tried to teach me how to drive, but it didn't work. It was one of the few times in our marriage that he ever said bad words.

I used to ask him, "When I learn how to drive, will I have to use your language?"

Chapter 18
Returning to Downey

After 20 years in Chicago, Tom was ready to be closer to the place where he was born. He still had 10 years to work before retirement, so he applied to work for the postal service on the West Coast.

One day he received a letter from Downey — the city in Southern California where I had grown up — saying they had one vacancy for a mail carrier.

We left Chicago in February 1965. It was a very snowy day and my sister Frances and her husband drove us to O'Hare Airport. My family did not want to see us leave, but it was time for Tom to be closer to his family.

Returning to Downey as an adult was interesting. Oh my goodness, everything was so different after so many years, I didn't even recognize it. Miles and miles of farms and orange groves had been replaced by houses, cars and roads. The landscape had changed so much, I don't know if I could have even located the farm where my family lived and worked for the Ikegamis for so many years.

We initially stayed for a week with the Tanaka family,

who we knew from Chicago, in their home near the Los Angeles Airport. One day while driving around looking for a place to live, we saw a mailman. Tom got out of the car and said, "I'm looking for an apartment. I'm transferring from the Chicago post office." Amazingly, the mailman knew of an apartment for rent upstairs in the building right where they were standing. We got that apartment. It was really nice.

Tom working at the Downey Post Office, where his nickname was "The Happy Hawaiian."

Things were very different in Southern California than what we had become accustomed to in Chicago. For one thing, Tom often remarked how much farther apart the buildings were while he was delivering mail.

We also had our car stolen. All our years in Chicago, we had never experienced such a thing. In Downey, we had a beige Volkswagen Beetle. I enjoyed riding in that car. It took us everywhere we wanted to go: San Diego, Santa Barbara, San Francisco. The only thing I didn't love about it was when going up a hill, our car could not keep up and all the other cars passed us.

On December 1, Tom was ready to take me to work, because I still had not learned how to drive. But when we came outside, our car was gone. On Christmas Day, the police found our Beetle in Watts. Everything was stripped, only the cab was left.

We replaced our beloved Beetle with a green two-door Ford sedan that Tom chose. We did not own it very long. One day Tom decided to drive it to work, although it took him only 7 minutes to walk to work. He parked it on the side of the road near the post office. When he came out after work, he discovered that someone had rammed into it. It was totaled, so again we had to look for another vehicle. The next car Tom bought was a brown, five-shift Ford Pinto.

After 10 years working for the Downey post office, Tom retired. At first he had no idea what to do with all his extra time. Fortunately, he made friends everywhere he went.

One day he met a Japanese man who was paralyzed from his waist down. They became friends, as they both enjoyed collecting stamps. Tom would carry the man in his wheelchair upstairs to our second floor apartment to have lunch with us, and the two of them spent hours talking about stamps.

Often Tom found himself at Winchell's Donuts, next to a small restaurant that was two doors down from the place I was working. He would sit for hours and talk to everyone who walked by, and to the mailman who delivered mail in that area.

Some of the girls from the store where I worked bought lunch from the restaurant next to Winchell's. They would come back and tell me they saw Tom sitting there, chatting with everyone. Tom got to know all my co-workers by name, as well as all the other employees of nearby businesses who frequented Winchell's and that restaurant.

When they saw Tom, my co-workers would tell me, "Here comes your husband with the big smile on his face." My lady friends told me that Tom was such a happy guy, that they could see him smiling, even from the back. I don't think anyone could laugh like he did.

Chapter 19
Learning to Drive #2

One day I saw a notice in the Downey newspaper about a night school class for senior citizens to learn how to drive. I decided it was time I gave it a try.

There were 30 or 35 ladies in the class. We practiced driving in a simulator made out of corrugated cardboard that was shaped like a car. We had keys that we had to take inside the simulator, pretend to start the motor and watch a film with roads, highways, stop signs, yield signs, people walking across roads, curves, going up hills, going down hills, speed limit signs and more.

I guess I wasn't doing too well in the simulator. Our instructor said, "Oh my God, Susan, you are a terrible driver. You are killing everyone on the road!" I guess I wasn't the only one having a hard time. The instructor told us, "This is the worst class that I ever had." Only one woman did well because her husband was a highway patrolman.

I also had the hardest time translating what I learned in class with our cardboard vehicle to our five-speed Ford Pinto at home. I won't even tell you the words my beloved husband said while he was trying to teach me.

When the class was over, I had to make a long drive on the freeway to get my license. That Saturday morning it was a very foggy day. I drove all the way from Downey to Seal Beach, normally 30 minutes, but in that fog, it took much longer.

I must have learned something because I made it. The instructor said I did very well and gave me my driver's license. But I still didn't like to drive and rarely drove anywhere.

Chapter 20
Ferndale Nursery

Across from the A&P grocery store was a very nice nursery named Ferndale Nursery. They sold tropical fish, furniture and beautiful pottery. I thought it would be a lovely place to work, so one morning Tom took me to apply for a job.

The boss seemed rather stern, and asked me all kinds of questions.

"Do you know how to use a calculator or run a cash register?"

"No, I have never learned how, but I could learn."

"Do you know anything about plants?"

"Just a little bit."

"Do you know anything about fish?"

"No, but I could learn."

Finally I said, "Well, do you want to try me?"

He hired me. It was the first time I worked for a Japanese man. He was *Nisei,* first generation of his family born in America.

I began my first day in the fish department. The store

also had turtles and lots of birds, including mynah birds that could talk. "What is your name?" the mynahs would ask.

On my first day of work, my manager, Masako, was so nice. She had a special five-gallon tank with beautiful guppies in it and also a cute catfish that cleaned the debris in the tank. I had never seen guppies before, so I watched them all day, how they swam around, how they had little babies. I found it fascinating.

Masako taught me that those fish only ate an amount of food equal to the size of their eyes, and that I should not overfeed them. I also had to learn which kinds of medicines to give fish if they got diseases. My goodness, fish are almost like humans! There was so much to learn. I loved it!

I bought a large book on fish and educated myself. There were hundreds of fish to learn about. Did you know that some fish lay their eggs in their mouths and are called mouthbreeders? I learned that from my big book. I also learned about hundreds of aquatic plants that are suited for aquariums, what foods the fish ate, how to change the filters and how to keep the right temperatures in the tanks for certain types of fish. It was fascinating to me.

I became so knowledgeable about fish that when people came into Ferndale Nursery they would say, "We would like to talk to Susan." That felt really good. How far I had come since my days of working in factories! I was making my own success.

Every day I could hardly wait to get up in the morning and go to work. I enjoyed meeting so many customers who were interested in having fish as their hobby.

I also was becoming a role model without even know-

ing it. There was one girl who worked there who was constantly standing with her hands in her pocket. One day she came to me and said, "Susan, the boss always tells me, 'I don't want you standing with your hands in your pocket.'" I told her, "You have to work. Wipe the outside of fish tanks, even if they're not dirty. Do something. Keep yourself moving. He's not paying you for doing nothing."

Ferndale was a 10-minute walk from our home. Tom loved to walk me to work, carrying my lunch bag. He also liked to pick me up after work. He came in right at 5:30 p.m. More often than not, I would be busy doing closing activities, such as covering the fish tanks. The other girls would tell me, "Susan, guess who's walking in!" He was always smiling and loved to chat with my co-workers. To tell you the truth, I have never seen a Japanese boy like him.

After several years, my manager told the head boss that I was a very good worker. The head boss came by and tapped me on my shoulder and said, "My manager tells me you are doing real well." I said, "You know, I want something better than a tap on the shoulder." So he gave me a 25 cent per hour raise. It felt good standing up for myself.

I worked at Ferndale Nursery for 10 years, until I retired.

Chapter 21
Tom's Homecoming to Kauai

Now that we were both retired, in July 1977 we fulfilled Tom's dream of returning to Kauai. He had talked about living on the island again since we had gotten married 30 years earlier.

It was hard to believe I was leaving my sisters, brother and Mom behind. (My father had already passed on 10 years earlier.) But it was all worth it, to see how happy it made Tom to return home and spend the rest of his life on Kauai. He adjusted right away, almost like he had never been away.

When I first visited the Hawaiian island of Kauai in 1964, it was so beautiful, with fields of pineapple growing on the hillsides, thousands of acres of sugar cane stalks blowing in the wind, and lush green mountains, all surrounded by the blue Pacific Ocean.

But living on Kauai was a different story for me. I had a very difficult time adjusting. I was not accustomed to the culture of the Hawaiian islands. It seemed I was constantly in a hurry at first. I was so used to the hustle and bustle of a large city. Kauai, in those days, had a population of only 30,000.

I also felt very different from the local Japanese population. As one of my few early friends on Kauai told me, "Your ways are different." I tried to reach out to the local Japanese, but I found them shy at first.

After our first year on Kauai, I thought maybe I should go back to Downey for awhile and see how things would work out. But how could I leave my husband, who I loved, and who had worked so hard to support Rachel and me? Tom would hug me and tell me I was not giving myself a chance.

Once I began going to Kauai Bible Church, I started to feel more comfortable. It was a small church, almost all the people were multi-racial, and several of Tom's old friends from Kekaha, the tiny town on Kauai's west side where he grew up, also attended.

The first day I arrived, the guest greeter gave me a nice *lei* (necklace) made of seashells and a Kauai Bible pen. The next day the pastor called me at home to say he was happy to see me as a guest, said a prayer for me, and we chatted for a few minutes. That was the first time a pastor ever called me when I was only a guest at his church.

Time passed, and after eight years on Kauai, I realized I had been enjoying living on Kauai. I said to myself, "Oh my goodness, I have met so many nice friends at the church and everywhere. I'm happy here."

One day, after we had lived on Kauai for 11 years, Tom and I were shopping on the opposite side of the island from where we lived, and I got a big surprise. I ran into a former classmate of mine from Downey Union High School, who was the owner of a store where I was shopping. What a small world.

Over time, I learned that the people of Kauai are so different from the people on the Mainland. They're hospitable, so friendly and very caring. The people of Kauai won my heart over.

At 60 years of age, Tom's health was good and he was able to do a lot around the house. That was a good thing, because when we first moved to Kauai, the yard of our home was a mess. We had built the house four years earlier, and rented it out until we could retire to the island. The house was kept in good condition, but the yard needed a lot of help.

Each day I worked an area of three feet by three feet. It was tedious cleaning out all the tall buffalo grass and other weeds to prepare our yard. We planted all kinds of fruit trees: avocados, bananas, lemons and oranges. We had a large poinsettia in the front yard, and I loved my cactus garden.

My cactus garden on Kauai.

After all those years of my parents planting and harvesting other people's property, it felt so good that Tom and I owned our own land. I wish my father could have seen it. I know he would have been proud, and glad that he came to the United States.

One day Tom told me, "I'm going to take care of the yard for you today." A little while later, I look outside and what do I see? He's lying on the lawn under the tangerine tree. He said, "I'm resting." Tom was always joking around.

He was almost always right, too. I am glad I stuck it out on this island. Kauai is my home now, and I would not like to live anywhere else.

Tom and me on Kauai in 1986.

Before we left Southern California, Tom had said to me, "Yo, (short for Yoshiko), when we get to Kauai, you have to learn to drive because you can't get around there if you can't drive." In those years on Kauai, there was no public transportation like buses.

So when we arrived on Kauai, he tried to teach me on a five-shift, and by golly, I just could not catch on. He got very frustrated with me. Still, after 30 years together, the only times he ever got upset with me or said bad words at me, was while he was trying to teach me to drive.

I asked him what I always asked during our driving lessons: "Do I have to use the language you are using when I learn to drive?" He said, "Forget it! And don't drive!"

Chapter 22
Kindness to Strangers

Tom was not only friendly to everyone he met, he was also a very caring person. It did not matter who you were. The best way I can show this to you is to give you a handful of examples.

One day a young couple was on our same flight from Los Angeles to Kauai. They each carried a backpack, had no suitcases, and said they were visiting from Switzerland. Tom asked them where they would be staying on Kauai. When they said they had not arranged any lodging, Tom put them up for a night in our home. I was afraid because they were total strangers, but Tom was that way.

The next morning, the couple left to go hiking and Tom and I went on an errand to Lihue, Kauai's government seat. When we returned home, our guests had packed up their belongings and gone, but they left a fresh pineapple for us on the little bench where I liked to sit on our doorstep.

Another time, while I was grocery shopping and Tom was waiting for me, a couple who was visiting the island asked Tom, "How can we find Hilo Hattie?" (Hilo Hattie is a popular Hawaii retail store.) Tom said, "Hop in the back of our car and I will take you there." When we arrived at Hilo Hattie, I showed the lady how to shop for Hawaiian shirts and *muumuu* (loose Hawaiian dresses). They were so grateful that once they were back home from their Kauai vacation, they mailed me an Indian dancer figurine from their home state of Texas.

Once three Japanese ladies spotted me in a building in Lihue. They said, "We have been walking and walking, but no matter how much we walk, we cannot find our hotel." When they told us the name of the hotel where they were staying, we had to laugh because it was a 20-minute drive from there! Tom told them to get into our car and we took them back to their hotel. After we dropped them off, we started to leave, but they kept waving at us to stop until they could find a key ring to give us as a token of their thanks.

During Christmastime one year, we saw a Japanese lady carrying several packages away from the mall, as if she was walking home. Tom said to the lady in Japanese, "Tell me where you live and I will take you home." She got in our car with all her packages and we drove her home. We became good friends with her. Both she and her husband have passed on now, but I still see their son around the island occasionally.

The last example I can remember — though there were so many more — was the time I was walking in the mall toward our car, and I spotted a Japanese lady we often saw at McDonald's. She was carrying bags of groceries. I asked her in Japanese what she was doing wandering around carrying her packages of groceries. She answered in Japanese that she did not know what happened to her car keys. Tom drove her home to find her spare key, but when we got back to her car, we discovered that she had brought the key to her former car. Tom drove her to the dealer where she had purchased her car so they could give her the correct key. She was so happy that from that day on, the three of us became close friends.

When Tom first began offering rides to strangers, I was nervous. I was still kind of shy at heart, and was not accustomed to going outside of my own boundaries. But with Tom, life was always another story. He had time, friendly words and the desire to help everyone he met. He was one of a kind.

Chapter 23
Apology 45 Years Later

Forty-five years after World War II ended, the government issued $20,000 checks to those of us who had been interned during the war and who were still alive, as reimbursement for our suffering. I was 69 years old.

Some people feel that the $20,000 payment was not enough, given the injustice we experienced. **But what are you going to do? War is war.** I have always chosen to view the payment as a blessing.

My mother gave her check to my brother, Frank, because he was taking care of her by then, and my sisters were happy to receive their checks.

My father would have welcomed the money, but the formal apology would have meant more to him. He never lost his faith that America is a great country. He always chose to see his life as filled with gifts, even though he experienced so much hardship.

It is interesting that one of the U.S. Senators who argued most strongly for the apology and payment, Sen. Spark Matsunaga, was a Kauai boy, just like my husband.

They were born the same year, only six months and 10 miles apart. I wonder if he and Tom had known each other while growing up. Mr. Matsunaga had been incarcerated at a concentration camp in Wisconsin, even though he had been a second lieutenant in the U.S. Army at the time.

I am thankful for people like Sen. Matsunaga who fought on our behalf. Most people of Japanese ancestry were similar in demeanor to my family. We found ways to survive and make our way in this world, without fighting back. I don't know if that is wrong or right. I do know that, for so long, this was the Japanese way. *Gaman*: to accept what is too unbearable to accept.

Maybe, thanks to people like Sen. Matsunaga, standing up for ourselves has become the new way for Japanese Americans to be. I hope so.

Chapter 24
Aloha, My Dear Husband

Tom did not like vegetables too much. Once I made a nice salad for dinner. Underneath the lettuce, I hid a couple nice pieces of broccoli. He said, "Yo, I told you I don't like broccoli." He loved his bacon and eggs. He could eat it three times a day. That, plus his fast food and colas, I think they ruined his health. After a certain point, his health kept going down, down, down.

On February 25, 1995, we were eating at McDonald's with friends who had previously owned that restaurant, when Tom's face changed color and he collapsed at the table. Our friends carried him over to our Toyota and placed him in the back seat. One of them drove us the two blocks to the Emergency Room at the hospital, as I still was not confident driving.

It was Tom's first stroke. He stayed in the hospital for 40 days and could not eat that whole time. He was fed through a tube. For the first two weeks, a friend drove me to and from the hospital every day so I could spend time with my husband.

In the meantime, another friend said I should learn to drive. She came to teach me every day for about 10 days, even on the weekends. She made me drive around the mall parking lot, and showed me the safest roads to take and the safest places to make turns. She was very particular, correcting me anytime I did anything wrong. I told myself, "I have to learn." And I did. I was 73 years old.

Finally I was independent. I drove to see Tom in the hospital every day. I drove for the next 19 years.

Once Tom came home from the hospital, he was able to eat and do his hygiene habits, but he needed to use a walker and a wheelchair. We also needed a helper to come to our house and give him physical therapy. How different this was for my formerly active husband, who had delivered mail though the streets of Chicago and Southern California for decades.

For about five years, we settled into a comfortable routine, with me doing more for Tom than I had before, but with him still able to take care of himself for the most part. In the midst of this, one of Tom's symptoms was very odd: the skin on his right arm was so thin that it would bleed a lot.

But then in the year 2000, Tom began falling a lot during his exercise, which consisted of walking around the dining table with his walker. He began falling even while walking between the chair in the dining room to the couch. I now know these were probably mini-strokes.

One October evening at 9 p.m., Tom went to the bathroom to brush his teeth and put on his pajamas. I was in the living room watching television. After awhile I thought, "My, Tom is certainly taking a long time." I went to take a look. I found him on the bedroom floor; he had fallen and could not get up. I don't know why he had not called for me to help him. I think he was trying so hard to do it himself. It was his second major stroke.

I called our neighbor across the street to come over and help, and he called 911. A fire truck and ambulance came and took Tom to the Emergency Room. Our neighbor stayed with me at the hospital until about midnight, then brought me home. Tom was hospitalized for a week. I went to see him every day. I was able to drive now and did not have to depend on anyone.

Things were dramatically different when Tom was discharged from the hospital this time. He was totally paralyzed on his right side. He had also lost his speech, and I had to order diapers for him. He was not left-handed so I had to feed him breakfast, lunch and dinner. It took an hour to eat since Tom had to chew his food very well in order to swallow.

But he was always smiling.

I would open the drapes in the living room every day so he could look outside and see what was going on. Even when somebody came every other day to bathe him, he was smiling.

Tom was the happiest person I have ever met.

Four years later, after a number of other hospitalizations for various reasons, including several bouts with pneumonia, Tom was hospitalized again for 15 days. Doctors told me he had so much mucus in his lungs, that he could not eat or drink anything. But Tom was able to smile. He made all the doctors and nurses happy with his smiling, too.

Friends came to visit him and to keep me company. Some even flew over from Oahu. One friend kept busy making origami good luck cranes from one dollar bills and gave many to the nurses. Another dear friend cooked meals for me at home and did all the dishes. She did not want me to do anything.

Tom was getting weaker and weaker by the day. The doctor said he could do nothing more, so I brought Tom home.

I think Tom knew his time was coming. He wanted me to hold his hand and drink orange juice with him and eat ice cream with him. He could not speak but he would try to baby talk to me. I think he was trying to thank me for caring for him all these years. Or maybe for the entire time we had been married.

Saturday night, December 11, 2004, before I went to bed at my usual time of 8 p.m., Tom was still able to recognize me and baby talk just a little. I knew his time was near. He would look blankly at the ceiling, as if he was already far away. His eyes were turning a little cloudy. I hugged him and said, "Good night. I'll see you tomorrow morning," just as I always did. He looked at me and smiled.

I got up at 10 p.m. and sat with Tom until 2:50 a.m. His head was cold. Although his body was still a little warm, I knew my husband had just passed away.

Even when he passed away, he was smiling.

In our 57 years of marriage, Tom brought me much joy and happiness. Until death do us part.

It is more important to enjoy your spouse while he is living. Once your spouse is gone, they're gone forever.

The hospice night nurse came over about 4 a.m. and she helped me dress Tom's body before the cab came to take him to the morgue. I dressed him in one of his favorite T-shirts given to him by one of our friends that said, "There must be a special place in Heaven for postal workers."

In the summer of 2015, a reporter for National Public Radio (NPR) called me and told me that Tom's name was on a list of World War II veterans that NPR compiled of soldiers who were subjects of secret experimental tests with mustard gas during the war. She said the government had been trying to find out how people of different ethnic groups would react to the poison. They were hoping to find chemicals that could be used against the soldiers of Japan.

One of the NPR reports said, "Mustard gas damages DNA within seconds of making contact. It causes painful skin blisters and burns, and it can lead to serious, and sometimes life-threatening illnesses including leukemia, skin cancer, emphysema and chronic breathing problems."

This explains so much about Tom's pneumonia and other lung issues that he had for many years, and also the very thin skin on his arm that I noticed after his first stroke, once I was taking care of him. Some mustard gas victims say their skin has been flaking off unnaturally since the time they were subjected to those tests in the 1940s.

During all our years together, I don't recall Tom saying much about this part of his service to the U.S. government. I do remember him telling me that he thought being one of the test subjects would help prove he was a good United States citizen. I also believe that as a soldier in the Army, he was not given the option to say "No."

I wonder what Tom would say now that these horrible effects of the mustard gas experiments have come to light. Maybe the only way to bear this knowledge is with the Japanese concept of *gaman*, accepting the unacceptable.

I can almost hear Tom's voice calmly telling me, "It's in the past, Yo. Besides, what else could we have done?"

Several months before he passed away, Tom told me I was still beautiful. No one in my long life has ever told me that.

In the Hawaiian language, "aloha" means "hello," "goodbye," and also "love." Aloha, my dear husband.

Chapter 25
94 Years Old and Counting!

Caring for Tom for almost 10 years turned into a lifetime of learning for me. Learning to drive at 73 years old, learning to pay bills, making appointments with doctors for all our health care, learning to cope with all the house repairs by myself, going on errands and marketing alone. I even learned how to use a mobile phone.

For so long I had been afraid to try so many things. I learned that once you make up your mind, you can do anything.

I have also learned that endings can become beginnings.

I lived in the home that Tom and I had shared for another 10 years. Finally, after visiting a retirement community on Kauai several times, I decided it was time to move there. I am now surrounded by a beautiful green golf course, I have friends from all over the country who also live in the retirement community, and everything is taken care of for me.

When I think back on my 94 years of life, I credit my father for setting a great example for our entire family.

Had he been a different person, he might have been consumed by rage or bitterness at many of the circumstances he found himself in that were beyond his control. Instead, he was always happy. My husband, Tom, was just like my father. Isn't that interesting?

While recently sorting through some of my belongings, I came across a diary that I had kept in 1942 and 1943, when our family had to live in the horse stall, and then while we were imprisoned at the internment camp in Rohwer, Arkansas. Almost every day, the first thing I wrote in that diary was: "Perfect day."

I showed this diary to a friend. She asked me, "How could you write 'Perfect day,' even when you were locked up?" All I could tell her is that I've been happy all my life. I thought that was the way we were supposed to live.

I didn't know what the future would bring, but my life turned out great. I had my faith in God all along. And I have always known who I am.

Tom used to say, "After I'm gone, no one is going to call you Yo." Well, he's gone now and no one calls me Yo anymore. But I know my name is Yoshiko.

Me at 94 years old and counting!

Other books by

Write Path

PUBLISHING

Bringing stories to light

www.WritePath.net